The Ghosts of Wrigley Field

The Ghosts of Wrigley Field

Gary Tillery

The Ghosts of Wrigley Field
Copyright © 2014 by G G Tillery LLC

ISBN-13: 978-1497362253
ISBN-10: 1497362253

Printed in the United States of America.

For Nancy

The Ghosts of Wrigley Field

Through corridors dark and echoing,
past empty seats of chalky gray,
a rookie strode toward the field
to take the moonlit pitcher's mound
on the night before Opening Day.

A strange wind billowed off the lake.
Stars gleamed down in a curious way.
He paid no mind. He had come to
the hallowed ground of Wrigley Field
on the night before Opening Day.

Confronting the vast deserted stands,
dugouts dark and bleachers bare,
he hoped to calm his rookie nerves,
subdue his fear, and rekindle
the fire that had carried him there.

He churned the soil with restless cleats,
kicked hard rubber, swept back his hair.
He shook his arm to get it loose,
then, gripping an invisible ball,
turned toward home with a steely glare.

The absent crowd to him was hushed,
all breathless for the coming play.
They feared the batter at the plate,
afraid he'd rap one through a hole,
drive in a run, and steal the day.

"Now pitching for the Cubs," he said,
"the kid who tore up Triple-A
—Joe Harper, Pride of Centreville—
brought in to save a one-run lead
on this perfect April day."

He angled in to get the sign,
then drew up like a panther, still.
He set his jaw, sprang quick to life,
and blazed a pitch toward the plate
that arced from inside out and fell

…to thunderous silence. No cheer came.
He straightened up in a soundless hell.
All he heard in the Near North night
was a rumble out on Waveland,
and the squeal of a distant El.

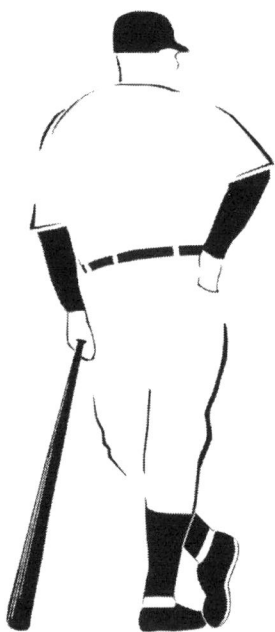

He felt a fool for expecting more.
The bright idea had lost its glow.
He found it now a juvenile whim,
one tale that he could never tell.
Even friends must never know.

Then he heard a throaty growl.
A gruff voice said, "Outside!—and low!"
Joe glanced to find the source, alarmed.
"Don't ever start behind in the count.
Not up here, kid. Not with a pro."

Now the hint of a shadowy shape
in the dugout rose to gray from black.
A face where none had been before said,
"Get the first one in for a strike,
unless you aim to brush 'em back."

The stranger stepped out on the field,
all manly shoulders, chest, and back.
His head appeared out-sized as well,
too large for such small legs and feet.
"Name's Henry, kid, but call me Hack."

Joe went cold to think of what
the man had seen—how much he knew.
No matter if he'd just arrived,
he'd clearly caught the humbling throw.
That was enough. That much would do.

"I thought I was alone," Joe said.
"No need to make a fuss. I'm through."
But the stranger, tilting his head
aside with crafty eyes, replied,
"Stay awhile. Word's around on you."

He seemed so strange, this grayish man,
with a uniform that looked a lot
like those from faded photographs.
What did he mean by "Word's around"?
Was he with the team, or not?

"I hear you've got a wicked curve,"
the stranger said, then spat a shot.
He took a stance beside home plate.
"Throw me somethin' I can hit.
Let me see just what you've got."

He'd grabbed a bat from along the rail.
He squared off with it now at home.
Was this some dark, sarcastic jest?
Hack seemed to read unspoken thoughts.
"No make-believe. How 'bout a stone?"

The crew had groomed the grounds all day,
as neat as with a fine-tooth comb.
"From where?" Joe asked. "The dirt's pristine."
Hack dug down in his pocket, deep.
"Use this instead." He tossed a coin.

It caught the moonlight as it twirled,
bright and tumbling, 'round and 'round.
It thumped against the rubber bar,
recoiled back toward the plate,
settled face-up on the mound.

Joe glimpsed the head of Washington
as he touched it, reaching down.
He had to grin. Did the fool believe
he could hit a quarter thrown
by the strongest arm in town?

Or was he simply having fun?
Haze the rookie? It had that smell.
Joe thought, *You want a whiff of air?*
and wound up for a big-league throw
—straight as a laser and thrown like hell.

Could be Hack had a jest in mind
—there just was no sure way to tell.
Joe came to life and burned it home.
The bat flashed out. He heard a *ping*
as clear and sharp as a hard-rung bell.

They must have heard that *ping* downtown.
That *ping* resounded through the night.
It shot so fast Joe failed to see.
A whistling phantom streaked away
to deep left field, clean out of sight.

He did make out a tiny spark,
like a distant firefly in the night.
His youthful eyes could see the spot,
above the wall and one row up,
near an aisle but to the right.

What in the holy name of Ruth!
No one alive could hit that pitch!
Ty, or Ted, or the luckiest man
in the world perhaps, but not this goon,
now using the bat to scratch an itch.

"How I miss this game," Hack said,
an opening Joe could not resist.
He walked to him at home. "You played?"
"My glory years were here," Hack said.
"Just when," Joe asked, "—when was this?"

"A world ago—before your time."
The way he said it sent a chill.
"They say you got a fiendish curve,
but that ain't enough, you know.
Anyone can have raw skill.

"You want to make it in the Show,
you've got to have a granite will.
This ain't the coddling minors, kid.
To make it up here in the Bigs
you need some grit. It's all uphill.

"It don't take much to swing a bat.
It don't take much to catch a ball.
What separates the boys from men
is the grit you show when your
back goes flat against the wall.

"When the count is two and two
and the next one makes you sprawl,
you got a choice—knock one out,
or charge the mound with fire
in your eyes and spark a brawl.

"I took no guff from *any* man.
I made 'em pay—you know the drill.
I charged a heckler ten rows up, once.
Thousands streamed out on the field.
Took a hundred cops to stop, and still—"

"*Aww*—give it a rest," a voice broke in,
startling Joe, and Hack as well.
Approaching them from deep right field
arose a shuffling silhouette,
friend or foe they could not tell.

Biding his time he must have been,
out in the bleachers, a rabid fan
too anxious for the season's start
to wait the night, made curious
when their dialogue began.

He walked to them with old, stiff hips.
"Is that all this game is to you?
This kid can make the Hall of Fame.
His curve will tie 'em up in knots,
but you'd prefer him black and blue."

He had a wizened, kindly face
of eighty-five to ninety-two.
"There's more to the game than blood,"
he said, "—even more than loss and win.
There's pride, finesse, and honor, too."

"Fancy words for a bleacher bum,"
said Hack. At this, the old man drew
up to his height of five foot six
and glared at the oaf confronting him.
"That's *Mister* Bum, to the likes of you.

"We deserve respect, my friend.
We're the spirit of the park.
When things seem hopeless, pointless, grim,
when a must-win game sinks into rout,
count on us to keep the spark.

"Sure, we hold our own team dear
—that's what fans are for. Even so,
we guard this fine old field like a
treasure chest of memories, a past
that's always near." He turned to Joe.

"Consider where you're standing.
Think of all that's happened here.
Take a moment, drift on back.
October first of thirty-two
—Don't you feel it near?

"We faced the hated Yankees.
Can't you see it in your head?
First time on top since twenty-nine,
when Philly knocked us out in five
—and this Series started bad.

"We dropped the first two in New York
before the guys turned homeward-bound.
Once they did our spirits rose.
They'd have to deal with Wrigley Field,
and Charlie Root up on the mound.

"The Yanks were tough, but our young gang
had been scrambling back all year.
When they put four up on the board,
our boys matched 'em run for run.
We drew strength from that Yankee sneer.

"And so the fifth began—tied up.
Charlie got the first man out
on a ground-ball chopped to short.
But then he had to face The Babe,
and the crowd leaped up to shout.

"Such a din you can't conceive.
Forty thousand throats let loose.
All day long they'd razzed him hard,
tossing lemons on the field,
showering him with wild abuse.

"From the bench our boys chimed in,
teasing, cursing, calling names—all
kinds of wicked, vicious taunts.
Focus on anything, they thought,
anything but that little ball.

"Commissioner Landis was here,
appraising what they had to say.
But the biggest shot of all
was FDR, only a month
away from election day.

"Ruth stood right here and took it in.
He'd clubbed a long one in the first,
a three-run shot that kicked it off.
Now Charlie had a single aim
—to make darn sure that was his worst.

"Sizing up his portly prey,
Root bore down and burned one in.
The Babe laid off a called strike one
and the crowd went wild, savoring
the sight of his chagrin.

"Then the Babe did something odd.
Like some great sultan in the sun
he raised a hand. 'Yes, I'll admit,'
he seemed to say, acknowledging
a mere detail, 'that's one.'

"Root tried hard to interest him
in two more balls just off the plate.
Ruth leaned in each time with care,
but he possessed an eagle eye
and the steely will to wait.

"Then Gabby gave the sign for curve,
and Charlie sneaked the ball across.
When the ump cried out, 'Strike two!'
the Babe held up his hand once more,
and here is where the stories cross.

"Some folks are sure he meant to taunt
our feisty bench, while some just *knew*
he aimed a nasty barb at Root.
But to my eye he pointed
at the flagpole, straight and true.

"Myth, or memory? Ask the wind.
'Still one more left,' he said to me,
'and *there* is where it's headed.'
To me he stepped above the game,
and rose on up to destiny.

"He'd done it in the past, you see.
You know—that dying Jersey kid.
Gave his word he'd knock one out
his next game up—a homer
made-to-order... Then he did.

"When Root uncoiled and pitched again
a mighty *crack* cut short the yell
in every throat. The ball soared high
above the fielders, caught the wind,
carried well beyond the fence, and fell

at the bottom of the flagpole
—four hundred and fifty feet
if it was an inch. It settled
in the deepest nook of the park,
a nun's-throw short of the street."

"The lucky cuss!" Hack intruded,
annoyed to be on ice so long.
"If he'd swung an eighth of an inch
above or below, that homer
would have been a bluff gone wrong."

The bleacher bum ignored him.
"Were we all furious that day?
Of course. And he made it worse,
when he rounded first, by jabbing
the air in a scornful way.

"But if you truly love this game
there comes a time to cut the crap.
Our world's a diamond, after all.
When you see a gem like that,
what can you do but tip your cap?"

Hack refused to yield the point.
"His back was to the wall, I say.
We'd razzed him to the bone until
he felt he had to take a stand,
tweak our noses, make us pay."

An unfamiliar voice replied,
"I think you miss the point, my friend.
Can you watch a glorious dawn
and care about whose side it's on?
—much less its motivation?"

From left field a figure came,
shouldering a wooden rake.
Said the bleacher bum, "Meet Ken.
He grooms these grounds by day and night
—too passionate to take a break."

Ken went on, "My ornery friend,
don't you breathe the air we do?
Who can begrudge the perfect?
Can't you see there's more to this
game we love than who beats who?"

Joe wondered as he lectured on:
Where had he been? Were there more?
Was Security asleep?
Himself, he'd hidden in the john
until he heard the last locked door.

"Sure, it's a test to prove who's best,
but there's more at the beating heart
of this game than lose or win.
What seems a simple pastime
is a craft approaching art.

"Baseball echoes life, my friend,
lulling you with tedious gray,
only to jolt you wide awake
with some dazzling, unforeseen,
irreproducible play.

"See a runner stealing home,
or a shortstop make a throw
no human in the world could make,
and the boundaries you accept
for what we all can do will grow.

"It's a diamond-perfect world
where you can watch, as on a stage,
real men grapple with their fate.
Will they fail, succeed, or achieve
a miracle like the Babe's?

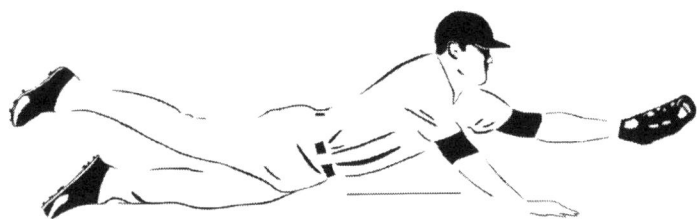

"This field is like a temple,
a place to contemplate, to come
and muse on the things that bind
us all—and that need not be
a mythomagical home run.

"I still recall that distant day
I first came here to tend the flame.
One of the crew was a fine
old gent the rest of us called Dad,
who loved to tell of *his* first game.

"This was back in the days of yore;
he was only a bat boy then.
The place was not yet Wrigley Field
—Weegham Park was still its name—
and the Cubs had just moved in.

"Cincy was in town that day
—Hippo Vaughn on the hill for us,
Fred Toney pitching for the Reds—
and about the sixth the fans
began to stir and make a fuss.

"Not *one lone hit* for either side
—both Fred and Hippo sharp as tacks—
and on and on the tension built.
Guy after guy stepped up and failed,
too quick to swing, or stiff as wax.

"History came to town that day
—*two* no-hitters into the tenth.
No fan could believe his eyes.
The odds were astronomical
—never happened before, or since.

"When Getz came up to try once more
the crowd grew silent, held its breath.
Vaughn retired him—drew a roar—
but with that throw his luck ran out.
Mincing to the plate came death.

"The little Cincy shortstop, Kopf,
choked the bat, then rapped a ball
that snuck between 'em into right.
That feeble single broke the spell.
No more magic—that was all.

"Greasy Neale popped one to center.
Williams never showed a doubt.
But Chase then sent another up
that Williams couldn't seem to hold.
Two men on and two men out.

"Chase stole second on a whim,
and there it stood—with two men primed
to score, the shutout still alive,
and brandishing his chosen wood
the greatest athlete of all time.

"Now Dad knew Indians only
from his grandpa's fireside tales.
They'd roamed the rugged hinterlands
in quest of buffalo and scalps
—in days long passed, on vanished trails.

"Yet here one came: Wa-Tho-Huk
to his people—'Bright Path' for short—
but known to every baseball fan
by the name the '12 Olympics
spread around the world—Jim Thorpe.

"In Stockholm he took gold in
both decathlon *and* pentathlon.
Beyond the rest, he seemed to some
like a modern-day Greek God.
Yet he was pure American.

"King Gustav, complimenting him
with regal grace said, 'You, sir, are
the greatest athlete in the world.'
Protocol meant squat to Jim.
'Thanks, King' replied the artless star.

"Six months later came the trouble:
Thorpe had once been paid to play.
They stripped him, then, of all awards.
But here's the thing: a man must eat.
Don't you do what you *know* for pay?

"And here's where it gets curious:
the rule was clear about the right
to challenge things for *thirty days*.
Is that a rule they'd still ignore
if Wa-Tho-Huk had been white?

"So here was Thorpe, all set at home,
with two men out and two men on.
Did he smash a grand home run?
No, sir—tapped a simple grounder
down the third-base side of Vaughn.

"Hippo watched him streak for first.
The fans saw Kopf and gave a groan.
With just an instant to decide,
and sensing Thorpe would beat the throw,
Vaughan turned to whip the ball to home.

"That caught the catcher by surprise.
The ball rebounded off his chest.
Kopf raced home the winning run
right here beneath our very feet,
and Vaughn saw bad luck spoil his best.

"Dad should have been upset; we lost.
But he took pride, from that day on,
that in the best game ever pitched
he had seen the great Jim Thorpe
driving in the winning run.

"Not a single medal hung
from Jim Thorpe's neck that fateful day.
But since no one had bested him
but bigoted authorities,
Dad could see gold anyway."

Joe turned homeward in his mind
to Jamie, one-fourth Cherokee
—an awkward fact in days gone by,
now an open point of pride, and
the source of her dark beauty.

They'd met in class at ISU,
soon fell in love, made plans to wed.
But once the scouts began to come
it made more sense to wait and see
—to let Joe prove himself instead.

A car horn blared on Waveland,
prompting shouts and peals of laughter.
Tomorrow afternoon, he thought,
they could all be watching me.
A shiver followed after.

The ten-year trail that led him here
could very soon come to an end.
He'd turned thirteen when it began:
Coach Egan heard a *whap* and paused
to watch him throwing to a friend.

He gave Joe some pointers then,
but more than that, a purpose.
Joe buckled down and made the team,
greeted every day resolved,
and weekly grew less frivolous.

He said to Ken, "Medals or not,
Jim Thorpe was one who got it done.
They knew his value in the clutch
—that he could throw and hit and run.
He was as gifted as they come.

"I have one gift, and that's my arm.
That's all I have, and with good luck
a year to show what I can do.
If I don't perform, I'm through.
They pay for value, not for pluck."

"I beg to differ," said a shape
appearing from a darkened row.
The moon that moment cleared a cloud.
It gave the stranger's gliding form
a somewhat pale and eerie glow.

He straddled the rail, then joined them.
Joe caught the scent, as he came near,
of mustard-laden hot dogs.
Why would they cook today? he mused,
but suddenly he wanted beer.

"You call to mind a long-gone game,
the biggest day we ever had.
Fans on every seat and rail,
craving beer and Cracker Jack.
We worked those rows till our feet bled.

"This was May of forty-seven,
and half the people in the park
had come up from the far south side,
sporting suits and Sunday dresses,
to watch a rookie make his mark.

"The Brooklyn Dodgers were in town,
and with them Jackie Robinson.
The man had class, I'll tell you that.
He heard some awful names that day
you'd not expect from *anyone*.

"The idiots were out in force,
without a clue of how it was
to live your life in disrespect.
He took it stoically in stride,
a man with talent *and* a cause.

"Curious how he did that day?
O-for-four—couldn't buy a hit.
Drew a walk but couldn't steal,
made an error, struck out twice,
left the field not owning it.

"His fans were cheerful, even so.
He came to play, not lift a bale.
He did his best and kept his cool
in spite of raging ignorance.
His goal that day: to blaze a trail."

"That's what I love about this game,"
said a fan from a shadowed stair.
What in the name—? Joe thought again,
Who let all these people in?
Are no guards guarding anywhere?

The new man joined the group at home.
"Jackie was just like you and me.
He had his skills, he had his fears,
and then one day he felt a call
—the chance to alter history.

"I learned about him from my dad,
who said he was beyond compare.
He'd bring me here and hand the
stories down until, with time,
we had stories of our own to share.

"Think of all the memories shared
by throngs of families and friends,
by all this city's citizens,
and even those who've moved away
but still preserve their link as fans.

"There's a power in memories
shared that merges and unites
the hearts of total strangers.
Games, careers, and seasons pass,
but the unseen bond abides.

"I had an odd thing happen once.
I was sitting in the stands
in that dreaded month of August,
when the dream you've nursed since April
starts to crumble in your hands.

"The Cards had built a daunting lead,
so I gazed up and down the rows.
I saw the hearty and the weak,
tall and short and young and old
—fans of every stripe and pose.

"Then I saw the whole great crowd
—a mass of faces lacking names—
passing through that time and place,
a web of strangers linked as one
by affection for the game.

"A boy in jeans and sleeveless shirt
rubbed elbows with a businessman.
Behind them stretched a row of girls,
Hispanic, Asian, shades of white,
and African-American.

"I watched a vendor being hailed
by someone distant from the aisle.
He tossed the peanuts twenty feet,
then waited while a chain of hands
relayed his cash in single file.

"First came mothers and their sons,
then a buzz-cut veteran,
next two teens in Blackhawks shirts,
out of place in a sea of blue,
and last the dad who brought them.

"Each one passed the cash in turn,
not even conscious of the way.
This park is more than just a park,
my friend. It stands for something true.
I hope you fathom what I say."

Against the city's vibrant hum
Joe caught the sound of clinking keys.
He turned to glance and chanced upon
a piercing beam and unseen voice.
"Tell me what you're doing, please."

His eyes beginning to adjust,
he saw a guard and thought, *At last!*
"I'm on the team. Tomorrow's game
will be my first, and we're all here
recalling Wrigley's past."

"Just who is 'we'?" the guard inquired.
Joe waved a hand and swung around.
He stood there stunned. All five were gone!
But where? he thought, —*in just a flash,
without a door, without a sound?*

He peered into the murky dark,
but failed to see the faintest glint.
He strained to hear the fading tap
of footsteps down a corridor,
but could not catch the slightest hint.

There seemed to be no trace at all,
until he heard—or thought he did—
a rustle in the dugout depths.
From out of inky black he heard
a throaty whisper: "Good luck, kid."

The guard stood by and watched Joe squirm.
He seemed alert, but slightly bored.
"Let me guess," he said, "—the rookie."
When Joe said "Yes" he loosened up,
"—who talks with shadows. Help us, Lord."

On Opening Day Joe came at dawn,
before the fans, before the crews,
before the men who brought the keys.
Wrigley like a siren called.
This was his moment, win or lose.

In fretful dreams he'd seen them all,
those strangers gathered in the dark.
A mystery how they'd disappeared…
Were they flesh-and-blood, or just a
reverie of the grand old park?

He dressed and went out in the sun,
savoring all that came his way.
He bantered with arriving fans:
"How're you feeling? How's the arm?"
"Will it be a 'W' day?"

A trainer rapping grounders
hit a ball that skittered past.
Joe turned around to run it down,
charging into deep left field
as it rolled on through the grass.

He picked it up, but on a whim
continued to the warning track.
"Can I ask a little favor?"
he called up through budding ivy,
to a man in a dark blue cap.

The fan seemed pleased to help him out.
He bounded up to check the floor
one row up and to the right.
"Let's bring it in!" the trainer cried.
Joe shot back, "One minute more!"

Turning back he saw the fan
stand up again and shake his head.
He thanked the man for taking time
and hurried off to join the team,
chagrined at having been misled.

Within ten steps he heard a shout,
"Hold on—could this be what you mean?"
He stopped again and turned to see.
The fan threw something near his feet
that glinted bright against the green.

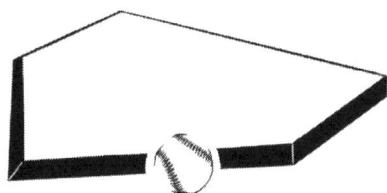

He felt a prickle up his neck.
The coin was blunt along one edge.
He reached down to pick it up,
afraid to think of what that meant.
He ran his finger on the ridge,

then held it in his pitching hand.
Might it bring good luck? Who knew?
Suddenly he felt a chill:
though pristine and gleaming bright,
the date was 1932.

Acknowledgements

I would like to express my gratitude to my wife for her patience, enthusiasm, and helpful criticism during this project.

Thanks, also, to Lou Cella and David Ives for reading the manuscript and providing valuable insights, and Jessica LoPresti for her technical help.

And a special tip of the cap to John Iwanski—the Wizard—for his superlative cover design.

Gary Tillery

A lifelong baseball fan, the author moved to the Chicago area in 1976, where he learned about the stately, historic, legend-filled edifice known as Wrigley Field.

Tillery's works include two other books of poetry—*50 Epiphanies* and *Through a Dark, Glassly*; three comic detective novels—*Death, Be Not Loud*, *To an Aesthete Dying Young*, and *She Stalks in Beauty*; and a collection of interrelated short stories set in Vietnam—*Darkling Plain*.

He is also the author of three works of nonfiction: *The Cynical Idealist*, *Working Class Mystic*, and *The Seeker King*.

In addition, Tillery works as a professional artist. He created the drawings used to illustrate this book.

His public sculptures can be found in Chicago, Hollywood, Milwaukee, Phoenix, Detroit, Sioux Falls, SD, and Green Bay, WI, among other venues.

His most prominent sculpture is the centerpiece of the Vietnam Veterans Memorial at Wabash Plaza in Chicago.

Tillery resides in the Chicago area with his wife and son.

.

Made in the USA
Lexington, KY
14 April 2017